COPIOUS

COURAGE

COPIOUS COURAGE!

MOVING - SHAKING
CONFRONTING THE ODDS AGAINST YOU

ROY ETIENNE SMITH, PHD

Copyright © 2020 Roy Etienne Smith, PhD

Cover Design: C Marcel Wiggins

All rights reserved. No part of this publication may be reproduced, distributed or transmitted in any form or by any means, without prior written permission. Unless otherwise identified, scripture quotations are from the King James Version of the Bible.

Dreamer Reign Media
P.O. Box 291354
Port Orange, FL 32129

www.dreamerreign.com

For Worldwide Distribution
Printed in the U.S.A.

ISBN: 9780997347708
Library of Congress Control Number: 2016903364

CONTENTS

Dedication 6

Foreword 7

Introduction 9

Chapter 1 Commanded courage 13

Chapter 2 Spirit of endurance.. 27

Chapter 3 Be still and know 41

Chapter 4 Cry, but don't quit.. 53

Chapter 5 Sweep around your own front door 63

Chapter 6 The one and only you..................................... 75

Chapter 7 Seven "tings & things" 85

Chapter 8 Success is deliberate 99

Chapter 9 Be a gold digger for a change.................. 109

Chapter 10 You can get there from here 119

Chapter 11 Overcoming fear and anxiety 129

Chapter 12 Courage to live, die, & change.............. 143

Scriptures in times of need 153

DEDICATION

This book is dedicated to my wife EShawnna, and our beautiful children. Also, to those who dare to dream big, and need BIG courage, I love, honor, and appreciate you!

FOREWORD

Regrettably, the world as we knew it has changed in a matter of months. When the Covid-19 pandemic started, I realized that things would never be the same. This is now the world in which my children will grow. The thought of living life now takes something more than a nonchalant attitude. The recurring destruction and devastation we experience on a daily basis is overwhelming at times. As I put my mask on before shopping for groceries, I am continually reminded that this is now our reality.

I used to hear older people make comments like, "What is this world coming to?" As a teen, I didn't really understand what they meant. I would just dismiss it as them being old and not embracing change. Today, I understand what they were saying—and often quote the phrase when I see the headlines of life. There is much wisdom available when we simply listen. When we hear about the mistakes some have made, and the victories others have won, we can learn lessons about health, family, and simply "life." A casual conversation sometimes can be filled with wisdom and knowledge proving to be invaluable time after time.

When we read and listen to bible stories of old,

various characters, and their experiences with an ever changing world, there is much to gain. The experiences of others inspire us to allow courage to work in our lives.

What do you do, when the world changes so rapidly that you don't have time to catch up? What do you do when everything around you seems to be so overwhelming? You trust, you stand! The bible says in Ephesians 6:13 "Wherefore take unto you the whole armour of God that ye may be able to withstand in the evil day, and having done all, to stand." It takes courage to trust—it takes courage to stand.

Dr. Roy Etienne Smith is the most courageous person I know. I once asked him how he does it. How do you go through "hell and high water," pain and pressure, then get up the next day as if nothing ever happened? COURAGE! As you read this book, Roy's words will show you how courage has transformed his life. Courage has strengthened his heart and cultivated an atmosphere of unwavering faith. Allow God to work in your life. You too can be transformed by Copious Courage.

—Dr. EShawnna M. Smith

INTRODUCTION
Copious (plentiful) "more than enough." Courage

When I was just a child, I remember visiting a Christian Book Store with my Mother for the first time. They had a large picture on the wall that said, "Faith, Hope, and Courage." I knew what faith and hope was. Nevertheless, I was very unsure of the word courage. I had thought about that lion that needed courage in a movie I had seen. Yet, I still didn't have a clue. I left the store that day not knowing, because I never did ask. A Psychologist once told me I had "big" courage after walking through abuse after abuse – trauma after trauma, but I was so full of anger and fear that I didn't connect the dots. It wasn't until I embraced the Apostolic/Prophetic call on my life that I realized there was more to this word and concept.

I was one of so many children who had suffered sexual, physical, mental and emotional abuse. For some it was a one-time event, but for many of us, it happened over and over for years. I am an overcomer, COURAGE comforted me. We moved from the projects to shack after shack. Some places had a furnace some did not. A cold bath tub was my bed on many occasions—being woken through the night as the toilet was being used. This was the same toilet that was flushed with the pee bucket when the water was turned off. I remember our meals of corn flakes with water, or powdered milk. If you got hungry at night, you got a cough drop.

I was rejected by my siblings, had no friends—I was the weird one, the crazy one. I was the one that was later placed in a facility for mentally & emotionally disturbed children and put on several medications until COURAGE calmed me. It allowed the super-natural to hit my life in such a tangible way. I was the same one who graduated High School with honors, SAVED, anointed, and in my right mind. I graduated college, got married, had children—COURAGE.

In my adult life, my sister died of AIDS, my mother, of Cancer. I was in ministry, rejected by my peers for abandoning church traditions for Kingdom mandates. I was lied on, sentenced to prison for something I did not deliberately do. I was supposed to plead not guilty, but COURAGE cautioned me. I was not supposed to fight this. I arrived at the prison only to be assigned to a cell mate that turned out to be my biological father I had not seen in two decades.

As a result, my Dad gave his life to the Lord. I was released in a matter of months back home by the Judge. There are so many miracles, and so many signs and countless wonders to even write about. Courage has changed my life. I have experienced near death experiences, sickness, homelessness etc., but to me at this point, it goes with the territory. If you want to trade in the good in you for the great in you, then you better be prepared to pay the difference.

We have much knowledge on faith and facetiously use words like brave and valor. Conversely, the comprehensive concept and ideology of courage is seldom reviewed. The world will teach you that courage is simply being brave in the midst of difficult circumstances. The church will evoke notions that courage is having faith - or trusting and waiting on Jesus to see you through a "storm."

Wait on the LORD: be of good courage, and He shall strengthen thine heart: wait, I say, on the LORD. (Psalms 27:14)

Most believers would stop there. They believe they have their answer. That would have been me. However, many years ago, I finally decided to ask God. My appeal was uncomplicated yet quite cavernous from the onset. "God, do citizens in the Kingdom *(Basileia)* approach "courage" in the same way we did in the world, or even in the church? He then began to reveal how copious *(plentiful)* courage really was. I found out its relationship to prayer and to outcomes that we desire to see come to fruition.

In a world filled with so much despair right now, courage is desirable. There are depths of racism, political dogma, and religious rhetoric running rampant. I thought Covid-19 was the virus of the year, but I'm not so sure. We need courage more than ever and I'm so glad that God has made it available in such abundant supply!

"Whatever course you decide upon, there is always someone to tell you that you are wrong. There are always difficulties arising which tempt you to believe that your critics are right. To map out a course of action and follow it to an end requires courage."
—Ralph Waldo Emerson

CHAPTER 1
COMMANDED COURAGE

Courage (Chazaq in Hebrew) means to be strong, grow strong; to prevail, be urgent, and to make strong. Courage actually strengthens your weaknesses that are submitted to God in prayer! Some are quick to say they have courage, but they are not growing strong, prevailing, have no sense of urgency and are too self-absorbed to make anything or anyone else strong. Courage wasn't designed to just give you some more strength. It empowers you to become strength to somebody else. We are gifts to one another!

Courage brings the seriousness and urgency of time and of seasons. It takes courage to discern the authentic voice of God. True discernment is not sensing right from wrong, but rather right from "almost right." Courage is a necessity.
Scripturally, there are various dimensions of grace upon the lives of God's people.

"As every man hath received the gift, even so minister the same one to another, as good stewards of the manifold grace of God." (1 Peter 4:10)

Similarly, there is a realm of courage that is not as shallow as we were once taught by the world or by the church. Discerning the depths of courage is of vital importance. Courage is not optional for the believer, it is commanded.

"Have not I commanded thee? Be strong and of a good courage;" (Joshua 1:9)

Know this about God:

Anything He orders, He pays for.

Anything He requires, He has already made it possible.

Thus, if He requires a certain depth of courage, He has already given it to you to operate in.

"... For unto whomsoever much is given, of him shall be much required: and to whom men have committed much, of him they will ask the more." (Luke 12:48)

It is courage that sustains us through our seasons of contradiction and seasons of turmoil. It is courage that provokes us to a deeper realm of prayer and intercession. It is courage that teaches us compassion, care, and concern.

Another thing about God:

You can't go underneath Him.

You can't go over top of Him.

You certainly can't get around Him.

There is a spiritual system to everything we do. When access is granted into the deeper things of God, it's not just because you danced or begged God—or started some prayer chain on social media. There is a certain grace that has been given. There is a password that unlocks things. God is of no respect of persons—but He is a respect of principles; relationship does matter.

When I stopped using courage as some watered down or plastic strength to get me through, my understanding changed.

"But also for this very reason, giving all diligence, add to your faith…" (2 Peter 1:5)

I added a new understanding about courage to my faith—and now I use it as my own driving force in prayer.

Courage Partners With Prayer

Courage and its partnership with prayer—keeps you humble in **Exousia** (authority-power)
It makes you bold in **Dunamis**, (creative-power)

It gives you wisdom in exercising **Dynamis** (resistive, yet resting power).

There is a courage that roars from within us. *"...but the righteous are bold as a lion." (Proverbs 28:1)*

Courage in prayer changes everything.

Courage in prayer produces much fruit and demands favor over your life.

Courage in prayer causes enemies and things you struggle with to be at peace with you.

Courage in prayer eliminates stress, cancels frustration, and tackles fear to the ground.

Courage in prayer reveals the character of men, the heart of God, and hidden strategies of your adversary.

Courage in prayer demonstrates God's humility, enhances our ability, and challenges every obstacle in your life.

Courage in prayer produces and releases strength.

| Foundational Courage |

You seek it—you acquire it. You use it when afraid and then put it away; a tool and a resource. During this stage of courage there is still hurt and a fear of people and their rejection. You are very critical of criticism and receiving rebuke is challenging. Courage is only a friend of prayer.

| Inspirational Courage |

It inspires others and brings hope. It challenges and provokes you to a realm of expectation; it stirs your faith; Valor is present and you're ready for a change. You can now tolerate the opposition of things and others. Courage is engaged to prayer.

| Transformational Courage |

You become courage. It transforms you for every new season and assignment. It releases the dimension of "trust" you need to quickly be obedient to the shift of the Spirit. It transforms others who encounter you. Valor is active and exploits are inevitable. You will welcome and celebrate rebuke and correction, and will have no issues in submitting to God's authority. Courage is married to prayer.

Destination: Exploits

Maximum utilization of courage = VALOR (heroism) Valor, (*chayil* in Hebrew) means a wealth of strength and efficiency (good organization and effectiveness) while using this strength.

Consistent maintenance of Valor is what births Exploits (an audacious or daring thing.) *"...but the people that do know their God shall be strong, and do exploits."* (Daniel 11:32)

   We sometimes see very little exploits because many don't possess enough valor. We do not have valor if we never maximize courage. Faith isn't always the issue. Many have faith but don't pray properly. Many have courage but don't maximize it. I always say, "What you don't know the purpose of, you will automatically abuse." We at times, abuse courage.
   Courage removes fear or anxiety of what is illuminated to you in prayer; it causes you to stand regardless of all odds stacked up against you. With

it, you can know the value of education and wisdom. You can keep your heart and motives pure. You can remain in the will of God—His season, His timing, and His care.

Bravery is not courage. Bravery is strength with an expiration date. It diminishes with every usage. Bravery is more mechanical and automatic. Courage however, crescendos and is transformative. Courage always requires conviction of the soul. Courage serves your anointing and your "Kingdom" assignment, and your walk with the Lord.

We don't understand courage as a current and a flow.

We fail to see how it expands and examine how it grows.

We miss the importance and its value to our daily walk.

We often forget or minimize it in our everyday talk.

Questions you should ask yourself:

Where or what is courage leading me out of and into?

Who or what is courage calling me to pour into in this season?

Do I use courage to only fight; or do I welcome it to also rest?

Do I mistakenly entwine faith & courage like others do with grace & mercy or church & Kingdom?

God is specific with each term, its policy, purpose and posture in the lives of His people; courage is no different.

COPIOUS COURAGE

COMMANDED COURAGE

Notes and Reflections

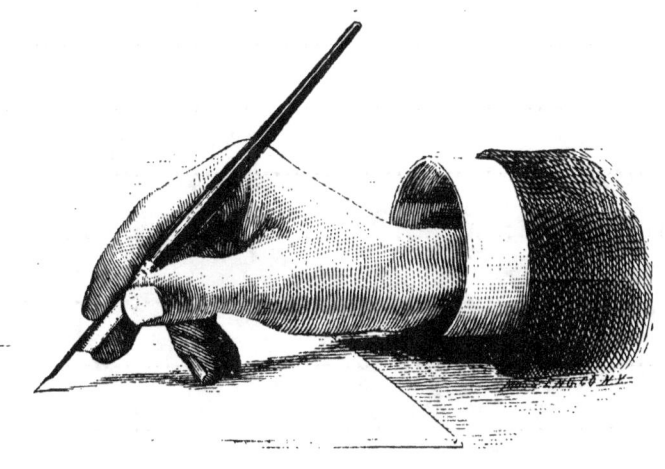

....
....
....
....
....
....
....
....
....
....
....
....

COPIOUS COURAGE

COPIOUS COURAGE

CHAPTER 2
SPIRIT OF ENDURANCE

Courage sustains true endurance. True endurance is not what we think. Maybe you, like numerous others, consider endurance the opposite of failure or defeat. Many times the word is used only in a self sacrificial way.

According to Webster's Dictionary, endurance is:

: The ability to do something difficult for a long time
: The ability to deal (regardless of pain or suffering that continues for a long time)
: The quality of continuing for a long time; to hold fast to

What comes to your mind when you think about the word "endurance?"

Do you think about not walking away from something or someone?

Maybe you, like numerous others, consider endurance the opposite of failure or defeat. The word endurance seems to have many facets to it—although many times the word is used only in a self-sacrificial way.

Joe may say, "I am not going to let this job do me in.

I am working almost ten extra hours a week without additional pay,

I have endurance."

Another person says,

"I'm going to stay in this abusive relationship because I have endurance;

I'm not a quitter."

The problem with both of those statements is that they are somewhat shallow. Although they both may point to enduring or "holding on" to one thing, they are sadly letting go of something way more important. They are letting go of their dignity, peace, and quality of life. Isn't this also the "what" that needs to be endured in the first place?

Honestly, I would rather keep my sanity vs. keeping score on how tough I was throughout all of the hell in my life. Our very own pride keeps us thinking to let go is admitting defeat. Nevertheless, if you held on to nonsense for years and let go of who you were in the process, is this not defeat? It takes just as much courage to leave a situation as it does to stay and "endure."

But you must ask yourself,

"What is it that I am enduring?

What am I trying to hold on to?"

Is it truth?

Is it faith?

Or is it a dead end street I continue to waste time wandering on?"

May God grant us courage to endure and anchor to attainable goals and great purposes in our lives—those ones that are worth endurance. For in this, you don't lose your God-given self in the process.

A philosopher once said,

"Some people are so loyal to people and things, that they betray themselves."

"But he that shall endure unto the end, the same shall be saved." (Matthew 24:13)

I always thought the "END" in this verse was talking about the end of everything, like doomsday. Everything is over with nothing else to follow. Nevertheless, the word end in this verse (*Telos*) is more expansive then final closure. Rather, the end of a process or termination of a purpose—meaning there is another process or new order or system that will begin. He is Alpha and Omega, the Beginning and the Ending. When something seems to end in your life, something actually just began. We only need to "endure" until the final part of "this" process.

The end is a bridge, not a wall. That is why death for the believer is not the end. We often say, the deceased has "transitioned." That is what an end really is, a bridge of transition.

> "It takes just as much courage to leave a situation as it does to stay and 'endure.'"

Fatal Distractions

Seattle Washington, a few years ago, a 19 year old woman was driving on the interstate—a routine trip she had taken numerous times before. However, on this particular day, she decided to take her dog along for the trip. The dog evidently was not used to being on the freeway with so much traffic and activity. He began to run back and forth between the back seat and the front seat. He eventually ends up on the driver's side. The driver became distracted by the continual movement and consequently ended up on the other side of the freeway and killed a man by hitting him head on. The dog took off up the highway immediately after the crash. (Just like the Devil, he distracts you with his movements, then leaves you holding the bag.)

However, the fact remains that she allowed him to ride with her. Sure enough, who she intended to be the passenger, ended up in the driver's seat and caused a fatality.

Don't allow anything to ride along on your journey that could become a fatal distraction to where you are trying to go and what you need to endure. Realize that anything or anybody that can potentially hinder or stop you from being all God intended you to be is an enemy. That being said, our own attitudes [or past for that matter] would qualify. I understand more and more this prayer of David:

"Unto thee, O LORD, do I lift up my soul.
O my God, I trust in thee: let me not be ashamed, let not mine enemies triumph over me." (Psalms 25:1-2)

See The Finish Line

One of the most rewarding sights a runner can see after running hard to win for several miles, is the finish line. If they can just see the line, it gives them the motivation and fuel to make it there. They know that at the finish line there is a trophy waiting. They long to experience the winds of victory blow across their face as they cross; as they achieve.

"Wherefore seeing we also are compassed about with so great a cloud of witnesses, let us lay aside every weight, and the sin which doth so easily beset us, and let us run with patience the race that is set before us,

Looking unto Jesus the author and finisher of our faith; who for the joy that was set before him endured the cross, despising the shame, and is set down at the right hand of the throne of God.

For consider him that endured such contradiction of sinners against himself, lest ye be wearied and faint in your minds." (Hebrews 12:1-3)

    When you can envision the completion of your project—or the outcome of your dream or goal, you can draw strength to pursue your triumph. You have to see yourself *"in it."* You have to allow your faith to give you a preview of what is to come. Sometimes even after you see a thing in your future, the reality of what is in your present is discouraging. Nevertheless, if what you "see" is not what you "saw," then what you "see" has to be temporary.

> **" Nevertheless, if what you 'see' is not what you 'saw,' then what you 'see' has to be temporary. "**

"While we look not at the things which are seen, but at the things which are not seen: for the things which are seen are temporal; but the things which are not seen are eternal."
(2 Corinthians 4:8)

When we focus on the end result, it strengthens our faith that it is possible. With our minds fixed upon the prize, we can endure through it all!

With A Made Up Mind

With a made up mind
With a made up mind
I'm willing to go all the way through
Though it cost my life
I'm willing to pay the price
I've got Heaven in my view.

If it means that I have to walk alone
Or that my friends they may be few
I'm not gonna worry about
What others may say or do
I've got Heaven in my view.
(Donald Vails, 1978)

SPIRIT OF ENDURANCE

When you are chosen, you endure (bear) truth. You must endure (carry on) faith. Your abundant life requires it.

COPIOUS COURAGE

SPIRIT OF ENDURANCE

Notes and Reflections

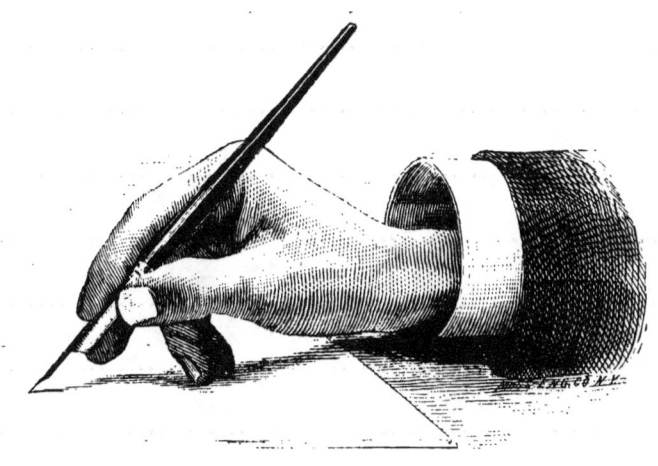

COPIOUS COURAGE

COPIOUS COURAGE

CHAPTER 3
BE STILL AND KNOW

I love the amazing miracle of the resurrection of Lazarus. Most only preach about how he was raised by Jesus after being dead for four days. There is something else within the story that is crucial.

"Now a certain man was sick, Lazarus of Bethany, the village of Mary and her sister Martha. It was the Mary who anointed the Lord with ointment, and wiped His feet with her hair, whose brother Lazarus was sick. So the sisters sent word to Him, saying, "Lord, behold, he whom You love is sick." But when Jesus heard this, He said, "This sickness is not to end in death, but for the glory of God, so that the Son of God may be glorified by it." Now Jesus loved Martha and her sister and

Lazarus. So when He heard that he was sick, He then stayed two days longer in the place where He was." (John 11:1-6)

Lazarus was sick then later died. Yet in the midst of the poignant news, Jesus "remained still" in the same place. Still is not just a quieting or slower stepping, but also a state of being. Regardless of the circumstance, you can remain in the same place of victory, faith, and courage despite the challenges you may face. If you were a giver before the world pandemic, be one "still." If you were a caring person before this storm, you can be a caring person "still." If you were a worshiper of God prior to this setback, you are to be a worshiper "still." "Be STILL and know that I am God."

"Be still, and know that I am God: I will be exalted among the heathen. I will be exalted in the earth." (Psalms 46:10)

"Therefore, my beloved brethren, be ye steadfast, unmovable, always abounding in the work of the Lord, forasmuch as ye know that your labor is not in vain in the Lord." (1 Corinthians 15:58)

"He that is unjust, let him be unjust still: and he which is filthy, let him be filthy still: and he that is righteous, let him be righteous still: and he that is holy, let him be holy still." (Revelation 22:11)

Circumstantial Bullies

When I think about a bully, I think about one word, intimidation. Intimidation is when fear is evoked by someone or something that produces weakness. Bullies will use strong influence to bring fear upon their victims. There are playground bullies that prey on other children on a playground. There are high school bullies who threaten the quiet ones or the ones who are not so popular. There are pulpit bullies who use their title or influence to impose their will upon those in the pews.

However, one of the most dangerous of them all is a bully you cannot see—but feel very strongly around you. This bully is a circumstantial bully. He uses our very own circumstances against us. It resides in the back of our minds and speaks to discourage us from success. Voices of the past, thoughts of failure and the like, all form this boisterous bully who can intimidate us to just slow down and eventually STOP.

You begin to hear its voice.

"If you try to succeed, 'this' could happen to you."

"Play it safe and stay in your cell."

"Peter, stay on the boat!"

"And straightway Jesus constrained his disciples to get into a ship, and to go before him unto the other side, while he sent the multitudes away.

And when he had sent the multitudes away, he went up into a mountain apart to pray: and when the evening was come, he was there alone.

But the ship was now in the midst of the sea, tossed with waves: for the wind was contrary.

And in the fourth watch of the night Jesus went unto them, walking on the sea.

And when the disciples saw him walking on the sea, they were troubled, saying, It is a spirit; and they cried out for fear.

But straightway Jesus spake unto them, saying, Be of good cheer; it is I; be not afraid.

And Peter answered him and said, Lord, if it be thou, bid me come unto thee on the water.

And he said, Come. And when Peter was come down out of the ship, he walked on the water, to go to Jesus.

But when he saw the wind boisterous, he was afraid; and beginning to sink, he cried, saying, Lord, save me.

And immediately Jesus stretched forth his hand, and caught him, and said unto him, O thou of little faith, wherefore didst thou doubt?

And when they were come into the ship, the wind ceased." (Matthew 14:22-32)

When Peter sank, I could hear the others thinking and saying,

"See Peter, look what happened."

Also saying, "We were wise enough to stay put."

Those who lack courage take the position, "If it isn't broken, don't fix it." Why? One reason is: Without courage, you will always be afraid of change. Circumstances will feed your doubts if you are not full of courage and satisfied with your faith.

"The brave and the courageous may not live forever, but the fearful and over cautious don't live at all!"

Can Your Change Be Challenged?

I believe God allows certain circumstances to challenge your change. Some say they have changed but when their change is challenged, they panic. I firmly believe that every authentic change can withstand ridicule and inspection like anything else of value. Once you have made up in your mind that you are going to fight, don't resist the fight once it has begun.

"Finally, my brethren, be strong in the Lord, and in the power of his might.

Put on the whole armour of God, that ye may be able to stand against the wiles of the devil.

For we wrestle not against flesh and blood, but against principalities, against powers, against the rulers of the darkness of this world, against spiritual wickedness in high places.

Wherefore take unto you the whole armour of God, that ye may be able to withstand in the evil day, and having done all, to stand.

Stand therefore, having your loins girt about with truth, and having on the breastplate of righteousness;

And your feet shod with the preparation of the gospel of peace;

Above all, taking the shield of faith, wherewith ye shall be able to quench all the fiery darts of the wicked.

And take the helmet of salvation, and the sword of the Spirit, which is the word of God:

Praying always with all prayer and supplication in the Spirit, and watching thereunto with all perseverance and supplication for all saints;" (Ephesians 6:10-18)

BE STILL AND KNOW

Notes and Reflections

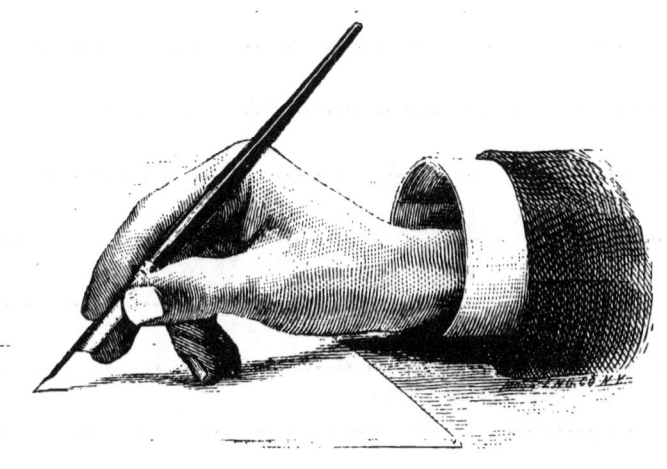

COPIOUS COURAGE

BE STILL AND KNOW

COPIOUS COURAGE

CHAPTER 4
CRY, BUT DON'T QUIT

One misconception that is quite popular is that crying equates somehow to weakness. However, some have come to realize there is a strength that is present when crying. Strength that acknowledges a challenge. Strength that recognizes pain when an overwhelming emotion is present.

There are many who feel once they are to the point of crying, it's time to move on. Others decide to give up, or rather try things a different way. If there is any strength or courage gained or realized through crying, then this should propel and encourage us to "stay" the course a little bit longer. We don't need to quit.

Crying is certainly far from our defeat. In many ways, it's the beginning of something way more awesome—Courage!

Did you know the average person produces up to ten ounces of tears a day and thirty gallons a year? While some are fighting to hold their tears, others understand and utilize their benefits.

1. Tears Release Toxins

"Crying does not only mentally cleanse, it can cleanse our body too. Tears that are produced by stress help the body get rid of chemicals that raise cortisol, the stress hormone. A study conducted by Dr. William H. Frey II, a biochemist and director of the Psychiatry Research Laboratories at the St. Paul-Ramsey Medical Centre, found like other exocrine processes, including exhaling, urinating, and sweating, toxic substances are released from the body when we cry. Several of the chemicals present in emotional crying are the protein prolactin, adrenocorticotropic hormones, and the endorphin leucine-enkephalin, which reduces pain."

2. Kills Bacteria

"A good cry can also be a good way to kill bacteria. Tears contain the fluid lysozyme—also found in human milk, and other fluids including mucus and saliva—that can kill ninety to ninety-five percent of all bacteria in just five to ten minutes. A 2011 study published in the journal *Food Microbiology* found tears have such strong antimicrobial powers they can even protect against the intentional contamination of anthrax. Lysozyme can kill certain bacteria by destroying bacteria cell walls—the rigid outer shell that provides a protective coating."

3. Improves Vision

Tears, made by the lacrimal gland, can actually clear up our vision by lubricating the eyeballs and eyelids. When the membranes of the eyes are dehydrated, our eyesight may become a little blurry. According to the National Eye Institute, tears actually bathe the surface of the eye, keeping it moist, and will wash away dust and debris. Crying also prevents the dehydration of various mucous membranes.

4. Improves Mood

Tears can elevate our mood better than any antidepressant available. A 2008 study from the University of South Florida found crying can be self-soothing and elevate mood better than any antidepressant. The shedding of tears improved the mood of almost ninety percent of criers compared to the eight percent who reported crying made them feel worse. Individuals with anxiety or mood disorders were less likely to experience the positive effects.

5. Relieves Stress

A good cry can provide a feeling of relief, even if our circumstances still remain the same. Crying is known to release stress hormones or toxins from the body, and as a result, reduces tension. Martin believes crying is a healthier alternative to punching the wall or "stuffing your feelings," which can lead to physical health problems like headaches or high blood pressure. "Crying is a safe and effective way to deal with stress," he said. "It provides an emotional release of pent up negative feelings, stresses, and frustrations."

6. Boosts Communication

Crying can show what words cannot express, especially in a relationship. This is mostly seen when a person in the relationship is having a different reaction to a situation that isn't transparent until tears begin to show. For example, "Someone may be trying to play it cool, or hold it together, or be out of touch with emotions—that are suddenly apparent when one person starts to cry," April Masini, relationship expert and author, told *Medical Daily* in an email.

It is at the moment one person bursts into tears that the flow of the conversation shifts toward the emotional aspect the conversation was covering. Masini believes "The crying can quell a fight, emphasize a point not gotten across in words—or simply underscore the importance of the feelings behind the dialogue."

A good cry or two can naturally heal us both physiologically and psychologically.

"My tears have been my meat day and night, while they

continually say unto me, where is thy God?"
(Psalms 42:3)

"I thank God, whom I serve from my forefathers with pure conscience, that without ceasing I have remembrance of thee in my prayers night and day;"
(2 Timothy 1:3)

"Blessed are ye that hunger now: for ye shall be filled. Blessed are ye that weep now: for ye shall laugh."
(Luke 6:21)

"And God shall wipe away all tears from their eyes; and there shall be no more death, neither sorrow, nor crying, neither shall there be any more pain: for the former things are passed away." (Revelation 21:4)

Notes and Reflections

COPIOUS COURAGE

CRY, BUT DON'T QUIT

COPIOUS COURAGE

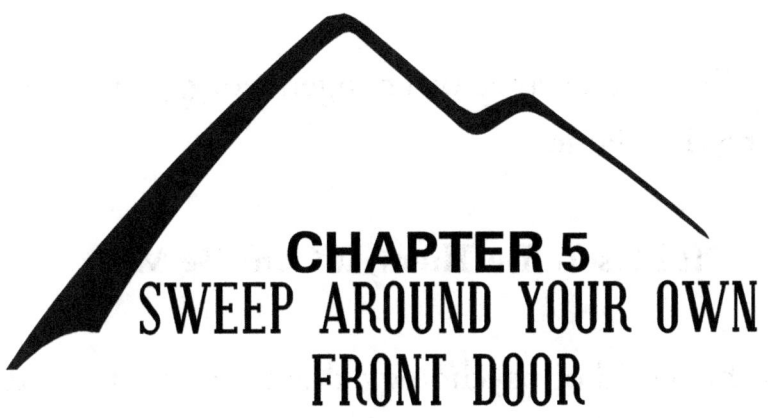

CHAPTER 5
SWEEP AROUND YOUR OWN FRONT DOOR

There was always a cute saying when we were younger. The saying was that each time you point a finger at someone else; three are pointing right back at you. Although true, there is a deeper awareness that needs to take place. If we continue to fail at taking responsibility and ownership in the things that should matter most to us, we will provoke others with ill will and wrong motivations to judge, correct, and mold us into their own way and mindset.

It is absolutely crucial that we handle our own affairs, failures, and successes with dignity and honor; it's cleaning time!

According to an article by changeme.org, people love shifting the blame.

"It Has To Be Them, It Can't Be Me!"

In the world of psychology, there is a word called "projection." When a person has uncomfortable thoughts or feelings, they may project these same emotions onto other people, assigning the thoughts or feelings that they need to repress to a convenient alternative "target." Projection may also happen to obliterate attributes of other people with which we are uncomfortable. We assume that they are like us, and in doing so we allow ourselves to ignore those attributes "they" have with which we are uncomfortable.

Projection also appears where we see our own traits in other people, as in the false consensus effect. Thus we see our friends as being more like us than they really are.

Example

"I do not like another person.

But I have a value that says I should like everyone.

So I project onto them that they do not like me.

This allows me to avoid them and also to handle my own feelings of dislike."

Projection is when an unfaithful husband suspects his wife of infidelity—or a woman who is attracted to a coworker accuses the person of sexual advances.

There are three types of projection:

Neurotic projection perceives others as operating in ways one unconsciously finds objectionable in yourself.

Complementary projection is assuming that others do, think and feel in the same way as you.

Complimentary projection is assuming that others

can do things as well as you.

It is important to perform occasional self inspection to make sure all is well—to make sure you are well.

"The most confused you will ever get is when you try to convince your heart and spirit of something your mind knows is a lie." —Shannon Alder

"Examine yourselves, whether ye be in the faith; prove your own selves." (2 Corinthians 13:5)

Self-inspection Checklist

1. What role did I play in this?
2. How can this help me be better?
3. Am I stable enough to move past this?
4. Am I overreacting?
5. Is my love, forgiveness, and my peace still intact?
6. Is my worship, purpose, and vision yet strong?
7. Can I see myself more than the other person or thing?

Man In The Mirror

I'm gonna make a change, for once in my life
It's gonna feel real good, gonna make a difference
Gonna make it right...
I'm starting with the man in the mirror
I'm asking him to change his ways
And no message could have been any clearer
If you wanna make the world a better place
(If you wanna make the world a better place)
Take a look at yourself, and then make a change
(Take a look at yourself, and then make a change
(Recorded by Michael Jackson, 1988)

"David, 'You' The Man"

I will never forget when King David had to deal with himself.

"And the LORD sent Nathan unto David. And he came unto him, and said unto him, there were two men in one city; the one rich, and the other poor.

The rich man had exceeding many flocks and herds: But the poor man had nothing, save one little ewe lamb, *which he had bought and nourished up: and it grew up together with him, and with his children; it did eat of his own meat, and drank of his own cup, and lay in his bosom, and was unto him as a daughter.*

And there came a traveller unto the rich man, and he spared to take of his own flock and of his own herd, to dress for the wayfaring man that was come unto him; but took the poor man's lamb, and dressed it for the man that was come to him.

And David's anger was greatly kindled against the man; and he said to Nathan, As the LORD liveth, the man that hath done this thing shall surely die:

And he shall restore the lamb fourfold, because he did this thing, and because he had no pity.

And Nathan said to David, Thou art the man. Thus saith the LORD God of Israel, I anointed thee king over Israel, and I delivered thee out of the hand of Saul;

And I gave thee thy master's house, and thy master's wives into thy bosom, and gave thee the house of Israel and of Judah; and if that had been too little, I would moreover have given unto thee such and such things.

Wherefore hast thou despised the commandment of the LORD, to do evil in his sight? thou hast killed Uriah the Hittite with the sword, and hast taken his wife to be thy wife, and hast slain him with the sword of the children of Ammon.

 Now therefore the sword shall never depart from thine house; because thou hast despised me, and hast taken the wife of Uriah the Hittite to be thy wife.

Thus saith the LORD, Behold, I will raise up evil against thee out of thine own house, and I will take thy wives before thine eyes, and give them unto thy neighbour, and he shall lie with thy wives in the sight of this sun.

 For thou didst it secretly: but I will do this thing before all Israel, and before the sun.

And David said unto Nathan, I have sinned against the LORD. And Nathan said unto David, The LORD also hath put away thy sin; thou shalt not die."
(2 Samuel 12:1-14)

COPIOUS COURAGE

Until you are ready to be completely honest with yourself, you can not be completely honest with others.

SWEEP AROUND YOUR OWN FRONT DOOR

Notes and Reflections

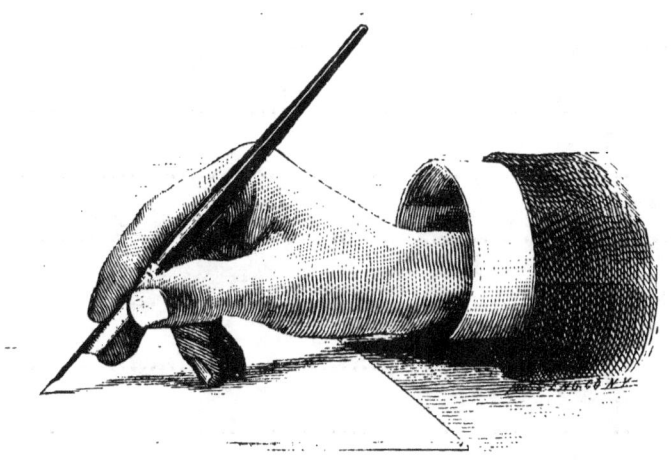

....
....
....
....
....
....
....
....
....
....
....
....

COPIOUS COURAGE

SWEEP AROUND YOUR OWN FRONT DOOR

COPIOUS COURAGE

CHAPTER 6
THE ONE AND ONLY YOU

Fingerprints are the tiny ridges, whorls and valley patterns on the tip of each finger. They form from pressure on a baby's tiny, developing fingers in the womb. No two people have been found to have the same fingerprints—they are totally unique. Identical twins can have similar DNA, but will still have different fingerprints.

Each individual is divinely made by God and has been given specific characteristics.

You may have an identical assignment, ministry or job of many others. However, you are still necessary—you are needed for the job. I remember being asked to sing a particular song at a funeral. I sat there remembering that the last funeral most of us had attended, that particular song was sung by someone else. I began to feel intimidated. I thought I should find another song to sing. With courage I still sang the song.

When you touch something, something different happens then when someone else touches it. The fingerprints of your life do not match anyone else. Yes, God called you. Yes, God needs another singer, another preacher, another teacher, another worship leader, another servant of God! Your very fingerprints are different.

"I will praise thee; for I am fearfully and wonderfully made: marvellous are thy works; and that my soul knoweth right well." (Psalms 139:14)

Intimidation

Dear friend, why are you so intimidated by others?

"They can do it better than me; they can tell I really don't know what I am doing."

Did they tell you that?

"No, this is what I believe."

Just because you believe it, does this make it true?

"No, it doesn't."

Have you considered that they are just as afraid as you?

"Wow, I never thought of it that way."

I know. You need courage.

Truth or Dare?

It is in understanding truth that can make you free from a mindset of insecurity.

"If ye continue in my word, then are ye my disciples indeed; And ye shall know the truth, and the truth shall

make you free." (John 8:32)

Truth is: I am an overcomer!

Truth is: I am more than a conqueror!

Truth is: I can do all things through Christ!

Truth is: I need to mature!

I dare you to believe God. I dare you to believe in yourself. I dare you to unplug any mechanism generating lies in your head.

"God knew what he was doing from the very beginning. He decided from the outset to shape the lives of those who love him along the same lines as the life of his Son. The Son stands first in the line of humanity he restored. We see the original and intended shape of our lives there in him. After God made that decision of what his children should be like, he followed it up by calling people by name. After he called them by name, he set them on a solid basis with himself. And then, after getting them established, he stayed with them to the end, gloriously completing what he had begun.

So, what do you think? With God on our side like this, how can we lose? If God didn't hesitate to put everything on the line for us, embracing our condition and exposing himself to the worst by sending his own Son, is there anything else he wouldn't gladly and freely do for us?

And who would dare tangle with God by messing with one of God's chosen? Who would dare even to point a finger? The One who died for us—who was raised to life for us!—is in the presence of God at this very moment sticking up for us. Do you think anyone is going to be able to drive a wedge between us and Christ's love for us? There is no way! Not trouble, not hard times, not hatred, not hunger, not homelessness, not bullying threats, not backstabbing, not even the worst sins listed in Scripture:

They kill us in cold blood because they hate you. We're sitting ducks; they pick us off one by one. None of this fazes us because Jesus loves us. I'm absolutely convinced that nothing—nothing living or dead, angelic or demonic, today or tomorrow, high or low, thinkable or unthinkable—absolutely nothing can get between us and God's love because of the way that Jesus our Master has embraced us."
(Romans 8:28-39 MSG)

Right Place, Right Time, Right People

When I was younger, I hated being in a room with a lot of people. Sometimes, I just wanted to sit there and not talk to anyone. "I don't know anyone," I would say. The truth of the matter was I didn't know myself. When you know who and whose you are, you can possess the confidence in understanding your necessity and purpose for being there in the first place. Time and time again, I see folk in the right place, at the right time, with the right people, but they don't believe it, so they sabotage it. The same individuals wander in wilderness after wilderness looking for something they already had and left behind. We often mistake being uncomfortable for some type of "spiritual discernment" that something must be wrong.

"It didn't feel right." They'll say.

When in fact, their mind wasn't in the place to receive it apart from the way they thought it should be.

"The steps of a good man are ordered by the LORD: and he delighteth in his way." (Psalms 37:23)

THE ONE AND ONLY YOU

Notes and Reflections

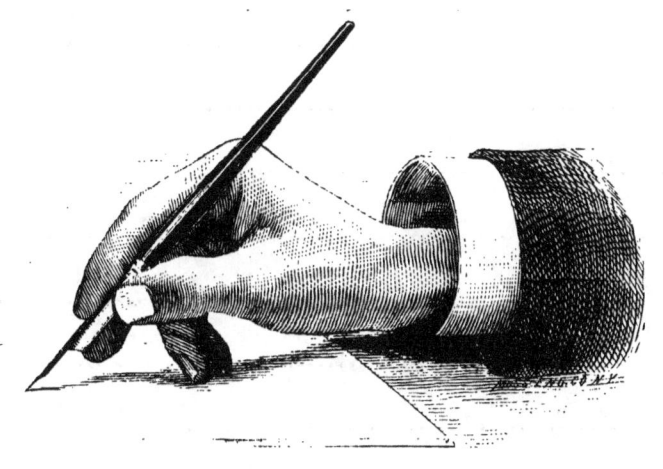

COPIOUS COURAGE

THE ONE AND ONLY YOU

....
....
....
....
....
....
....
....
....
....
....
....
....
....
....
....
....
....
....
....
....
....

COPIOUS COURAGE

CHAPTER 7
SEVEN "TINGS & THINGS"

I visited a Jamaican restaurant for lunch one afternoon. On the right side of the menu they had a list of side items. They called these items Tings & Things. There were (7) of them. In my first book over 10 years ago, I had dedicated an entire section with a series of 7 things. When I saw the menu items, it reminded me of some of the (tings) I had written.

I thought it crucial to record them again in this particular chapter of this book.

7 Things A Test Will Reveal

Real From Fiction, And True Authenticity

"Prove thy servants, I beseech thee, ten days; and let them give us pulse to eat, and water to drink. Then let our countenances be looked upon before thee, and the countenance of the children that eat of the portion of the king's meat: and as thou seest, deal with thy servants." (Daniel 1:12-13)

Hidden Things Never Hidden From You, Always Hidden For You

"That their hearts might be comforted, being knit together in love, and unto all riches of the full assurance of understanding, to the acknowledgement of the mystery of God, and of the Father, and of Christ; In whom are hid all the treasures of wisdom and knowledge." (Colossians 2:3)

"And I will give thee the treasures of darkness, and

hidden riches of secret places, that thou mayest know that I, the LORD, which call thee by thy name, am the God of Israel." (Isaiah 45:3)

Motives, Yours, His, And Your Enemy

"I will use them to test Israel and see whether they will keep the way of the LORD and walk in it as their forefathers did." (Judges 2:22 NIV)

"Bring the whole tithe into the storehouse, that there may be food in my house. Test me in this," says the LORD Almighty, "and see if I will not throw open the floodgates of heaven and pour out so much blessing that you will not have room enough for it." (Malachi 3:10)

Discipline Or The Lack Thereof

Examine yourselves, whether ye be in the faith; prove your own selves. Know ye not your own selves, how that Jesus Christ is in you, except ye be reprobates? (2 Corinthians 13:5)

Your Level Of Comprehension Into The Things Of God

"Do not conform any longer to the pattern of this world, but be transformed by the renewing of your mind. Then you will be able to test and approve what God's will is— his good, pleasing and perfect will." (Romans 12:2 NIV)

Your Grade In Commitment Of Your Heart

"Examine me, O LORD, and prove me; try my reins and my heart." (Psalms 26:2)

The Strength Of Your Character Which Determines Your Longevity

"Wherefore I beseech you that ye would confirm your love toward him. For to this end also did I write, that I might know the proof of you, whether ye be obedient in all things." (2 Corinthians 2:8-9)

7 Things A Trial Will Accomplish

Acknowledgment Of The True And Living God

"Hear me, O LORD, hear me, that this people may know that thou art the LORD God, and that thou hast turned their heart back again. Then the fire of the LORD fell, and consumed the burnt sacrifice, and the wood, and the stones, and the dust, and licked up the water that was in the trench. And when all the people saw it, they fell on their faces: and they said, The LORD, he is the God; the LORD, he is the God."
(I Kings 18:37-39)

"Then Nebuchadnezzar spake, and said, Blessed be the God of Shadrach, Meshach, and Abednego, who hath sent his angel, and delivered his servants that trusted in him, and have changed the king's word, and yielded their bodies, that they might not serve nor worship any god, except their own God." (Daniel 3:28)

A Major Decision To Be Made

"But ye have a custom, that I should release unto you one at the passover: will ye therefore that I release unto you the King of the Jews?" (John 18:39)

Confirmation That You Are Called Of God

"And after a while came unto him they that stood by, and said to Peter, Surely thou also art one of them; for thy speech betrayeth thee." (Matthew 26:73)

"And others had trial of cruel mockings and scourgings, yea, moreover of bonds and imprisonment:" (Hebrews 11:36)

The Exact Measure Of Your Faith

"That the trial of your faith, being much more precious than of gold that perisheth, though it be tried with fire, might be found unto praise and honour and glory at the appearing of Jesus Christ:" (I Peter 1:17)

The Amount Of Compassion You Are Working With

"And when she had opened it, she saw the child: and, behold, the babe wept. And she had compassion on him, and said, This is one of the Hebrews' children." (Exodus 2:6)

The Changing Of Your Heart's Desires

"Brethren, my heart's desire and prayer to God for Israel is, that they might be saved." (Romans 10:1)

"And God said to Solomon, Because this was in thine heart, and thou hast not asked riches, wealth, or honor, nor the life of thine enemies, neither yet hast asked long life; but hast asked wisdom and knowledge for thyself, that thou mayest judge my people, over whom I have made thee king:" (2 Chronicles 1:11)

The Seeking Of More Wisdom

"I applied mine heart to know, and to search, and to seek out wisdom, and the reason of things, and to know the wickedness of folly, even of foolishness and madness:" (Ecclesiastes 7:25)

7 Things Sufferings Can Bring Into Your Life

Consistent Seasons Of Divine Favor And Appointments

"Then Esther the queen answered and said, If I have

found favour in thy sight, O king, and if it please the king, let my life be given me at my petition, and my people at my request:" (Esther 7:13)

Generational Blessings You Didn't Know Were There

"And that I also have walked contrary unto them, and have brought them into the land of their enemies; if then their uncircumcised hearts be humbled, and they then accept of the punishment of their iniquity: Then will I remember my covenant with Jacob, and also my covenant with Isaac, and also my covenant with Abraham will I remember; and I will remember the land." (Leviticus 26:41-43)

The Revealed Glory Of The Lord

"For I reckon that the sufferings of this present time are not worthy to be compared with the glory which shall be revealed in us." (Romans 8:18)

A Spirit Of Repentance And Forgiveness

"For godly sorrow worketh repentance to salvation not to be repented of: but the sorrow of the world worketh death." (2 Corinthians 7:10)

Great Depth And Heights Into The Things Of God

"That he would grant you, according to the riches of his glory, to be strengthened with might by his Spirit in the inner man; That Christ may dwell in your hearts by faith; that ye, being rooted and grounded in love, May be able to comprehend with all saints what is the breadth, and length, and depth, and height; And to know the love of Christ, which passeth knowledge, that ye might be filled with all the fulness of God." (Ephesians 3:16-19)

Those Truly Assigned To You

"And the Lord said unto him, Arise, and go into the street which is called Straight, and enquire in the house of Judas for one called Saul, of Tarsus: for, behold, he prayeth," (Acts 9:11)

Uncommon Miracles And Restoration

"For thou, O God, hast proved us: thou hast tried us, as silver is tried. Thou broughtest us into the net; thou laidst affliction upon our loins. Thou hast caused men to ride over our ads; we went through fire and through water: but thou broughtest us out into a wealthy place." (Psalms 66:10-12)

SEVEN "TINGS & THINGS"
Notes and Reflections

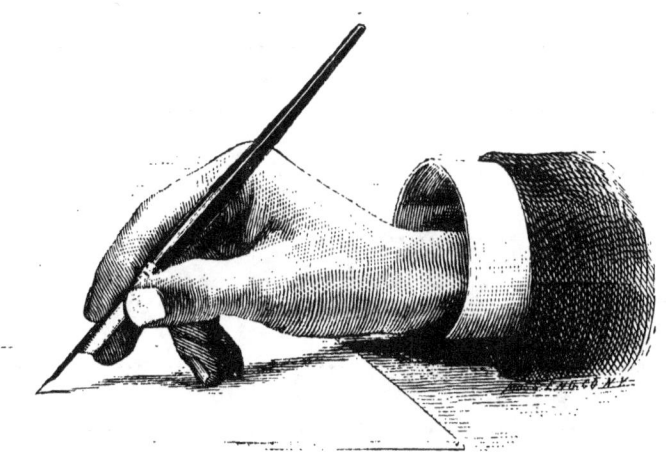

COPIOUS COURAGE

SEVEN "TINGS & THINGS"

COPIOUS COURAGE

CHAPTER 8
SUCCESS IS DELIBERATE

We have heard it said, "Success is not a destination, but a continual journey." I believe this is true. I know there are those who feel what is meant to be shall be. In church we had a song that said, "What God has for me, it is for me." While both of these statements contain truth, it is imperative that we explore the other facets of success. There is a facet of success that is very deliberate. I understood this when I realized that love is more than an emotion, it is also a choice.

When we take responsibility for our part of the processes of our life, we can obtain a depth of success that is not only achieved, but also maintained.

"For it is God which worketh in you both to will and to do of his good pleasure.

Do all things without murmurings and disputings: That ye may be blameless and harmless, the sons of God, without rebuke, in the midst of a crooked and perverse nation, among whom ye shine as lights in the world;

Holding forth the word of life; that I may rejoice in the day of Christ, that I have not run in vain, neither laboured in vain." (Philippians 2:13-16)

Failure On A Loop

Unfortunately, some of us have had more experience with failure than success. When things seem to be going too good or well, then we start looking for the worst. We learned to set our clocks by it.

We say to ourselves,

"It's only a matter of time before this all comes to an end."

"What's the catch?"

"If it's too good to be true, then it probably is."

I thought I had proven this theory based on my track record and the patterns of my life. I had no idea that because of an initial set of traumas, I actually had failure on a loop. It was coming from within me. I attracted it like a magnet. Trauma had damaged me emotionally to the point I felt out of control. Thus, having a pattern on a loop—I knew what to expect. When things were challenging the pattern and dysfunctional flow, I would be concerned. My concern was not that I really felt things should turn ugly. Rather, that I was not in control. Without control, I couldn't prevent hurt. Without control, I couldn't prevent pain. Some need failure on a loop so they can be prepared for each cycle they know like a book.

As we renew our minds and relinquish the control, God's purpose can shine through. It is no longer then what God can do for us, or in us, but rather what we are willing to allow Him to do through us.

"So here's what I want you to do, God helping you: Take your everyday, ordinary life—your sleeping, eating, going-to-work, and walking-around life—and place it before God as an offering. Embracing what God does for you is the best thing you can do for Him. Don't become so well-adjusted to your culture that you fit into it without even thinking. Instead, fix your attention on God. You'll be changed from the inside out. Readily recognize what he wants from you, and quickly respond to it. Unlike the culture around you, always dragging you down to its level of immaturity, God brings the best out of you, develops well-formed maturity in you.

I'm speaking to you out of deep gratitude for all that God has given me, and especially as I have responsibilities in relation to you. Living then, as every one of you does, in pure grace, it's important that you not misinterpret yourselves as people who are bringing this goodness to God. No, God brings it all to you. The only accurate way to understand ourselves is by what God is and by what he does for us, not by what we are and what we do for him. (Romans 12:1-3 MSG)

Are You A Believer?

Break the cycle of failure by setting goals and doing the work. Aim for your target. Walk in a level of maturity that realizes it may get worse before it gets better. We must be willing to hurt, take risk, and sacrifice so much in the pursuit. It will be worth the time. It will be worth the pain. It will be worth the wait. Those who want and need it NOW are immature. They will do whatever to have it now. Some may actually get it now, or the appearance thereof. Only thing is, they won't be able to keep it. If you stressed yourself out to get it, you'll have to stress yourself out to keep it. Whatever you did to obtain it, is the same thing required to keep it.

What is your strategy?

What is your plan?

Some have prayed, but no plan of action. Some have a "good idea," but no resources. Church people are known for being lazy and prideful. We think we can just pray, cry, and beg, then something will happen. Others feel everything amazing is automatically supposed to happen for them for some reason. Another population will recite scriptures like spells or some sort of "mojo." The truly successful individual understands process. They know timing. They know seasons. They know when to pray, when to speak the Word of God, when to wait, when to do nothing, and when to implement strategies with the wisdom of God. Do you want to be a true believer? Then, you must believe in the process just as much as the promise.

SUCCESS IS DELIBERATE

Notes and Reflections

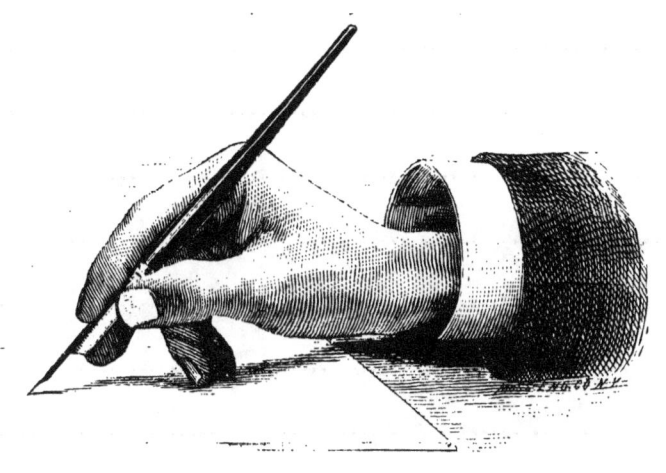

....
....
....
....
....
....
....
....
....
....
....
....
....

COPIOUS COURAGE

COPIOUS COURAGE

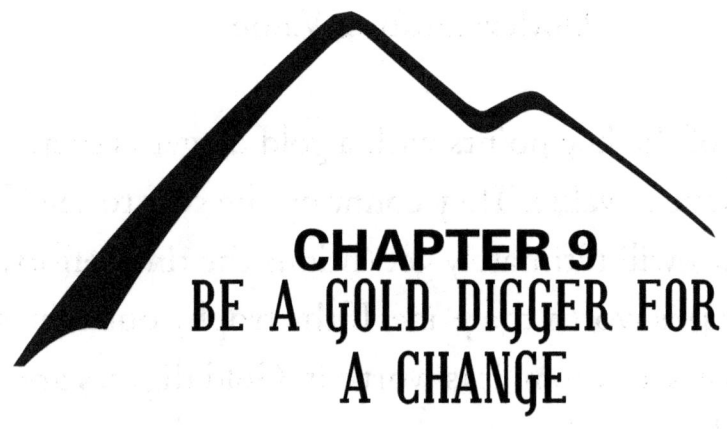

CHAPTER 9
BE A GOLD DIGGER FOR A CHANGE

Many have heard countless stories of young girls pursuing relationships with much older men. They are not seeking love—nor are they seeking any type of long term commitment. The bottom line, they just want his money. The term used very often to describe the familiar hustle is "gold digger." A gold digger's goal and aim is to get the "gold" at all cost. They do not concern themselves with anything that is not a part of the hustle. For them, there is no time to waste on things that do not matter—things that won't bring them any closer to their destination.

Understanding Value

One of the key points with a gold digger is their assessment of value. They count up the cost to see if what they will ultimately get (minus the time, effort, and risks) is worth the prize. If the trophy out values the process, to them, it is worth it. Gold diggers are not all the same. You may have one who desires cash. Another may just need power. For most of us, we desire knowledge. If we can learn from a situation, the education can help us be better without becoming bitter. It can further aid our endeavors of reaching our destinies on time.

"What is the value of this situation?"

"What did I learn?"

"How can I be better as a result of it?"

"How has it positioned me for the greater?"

"For which of you, intending to build a tower, sitteth not down first, and counteth the cost, whether he have sufficient to finish it?" (Luke 14:28)

The Plot Thickens

The gold digger must have tunnel vision. Their focus is not on cosmetics. They are not concerned about looks. They could care less about age. They know they are about to cash in if they just wait it out.

You cannot focus on how a situation may appear at the moment. There is value in it. Get the gold. I saw a gold digger on the beach once following men who got out of expensive convertibles and cars. She would ask for directions or ask about the car. She would talk about whatever she could to engage them into conversation. She didn't ask me anything—I was driving a Honda at the time. Her thoughts were:

"I didn't come to relax.

I could care less about how pretty the water is now. It doesn't matter about the warm sun, or the wonderful people playing and surfing in the ocean.

I came for the Gold."

Just like an old woman at a yard sale. She is looking for things of value to take home. Others may just see junk, she will find the gold. She knows what she is looking for and how to find it. She will move boxes, go through bins, and get her hands dirty making sure she leaves with something of value.

"Ask, and it shall be given you; seek, and ye shall find; knock, and it shall be opened unto you:" (Matthew 7:7)

Extract The Gold

Once you obtain what it is that you were to obtain from it. Properly distribute it—make it an investment into your life and future. Breathe then, repeat the process! It is amazing, this is how God sees folk that others do not value. Others think we are junk and why is God involved with us in the first place. Well, God is a Gold Digger. He doesn't care how we look.

He is after something greater He knows is there.

However, this Gold Digger wants a relationship, desires a commitment with us that He can continually access the gold in us as He makes available to us the gold in Him.

But he knoweth the way that I take: when he hath tried me, I shall come forth as gold. (Job 23:10)

BE A GOLD DIGGER FOR A CHANGE

Notes and Reflections

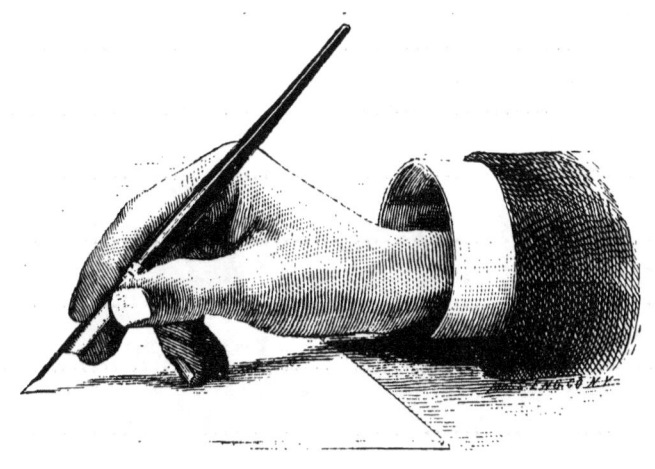

COPIOUS COURAGE

BE A GOLD DIGGER FOR A CHANGE

COPIOUS COURAGE

CHAPTER 10
YOU CAN GET THERE FROM HERE

There are processes in everyday life that point to something real and greater. Even in our car or phones, we have GPS systems that every hour, minute, and second, they calculate and navigate us to and from destinations. One thing you must appreciate is that the system will automatically begin to recalculate steps once there was a break in any way with the original pattern of navigation. It could be a mistake you made. It could be a sudden change in the traffic or weather pattern. It will direct you with the most current information available. There have been times in life when all our steps have needed recalculation.

Complexity vs. Simplicity

I have found when life gets most complicated it's not further complication that is needed, but rather something basic. Someone recently told me that we often master the complex, but we fail to master the simple. (Simplicity)

You may ask, "Now what?"

Good question!

It's time we realize some crucial things about life. One is that vantage point and perception play an incredible role in everything.

How do you see yourself?

How do you see others?
What is your view from the top?

Or even from the bottom for that matter?

Different - but true, some have a view from the side. Every position, although not necessarily your own, plays a part. When I was in college, I had an apartment and lived on the 10th floor. One night I heard much noise. I thought it was coming from underneath me. It was actually coming from above me.

I said to myself,

"One man's ceiling is another man's floor."

If we can only learn to respect one another's position and vantage point, we can complement each other instead of competing.

Courage To Try Again

If you need to rest in this saga called life, learn some rules first.

1. Stop Pulling Off The Side Of The Road And Turning The Engine Off.

You can pause; you can stop sometime—but keep that engine in motion. When you get your word of release or instruction, there will be nothing to "crank up." You will already be in position and in motion.

2. When You Rest, Keep The Vision You Have Moving In Your Spirit.

Have courage to rest your body and mind but never your heart. Never forget where you are, and where you just came from.

3. Cast Down All Imaginations That Speak To Your Mind.

You know what's right. You know how to move forward. Immediately eliminate voices that are contrary to truth. Draw your sword and fight. Do not reason with a lie. When you come into agreement with truth, you will be able to hear and see things the way they are supposed to be seen.

4. Use The Faith He Gave You, Quit Asking For More!

We waste much time asking for things we already have. In the middle of a fight you are more equipped than you realize. God only allows testing on your level of warfare. You have what it takes if you just use it. Quit spending countless hours trying to figure out why you have to "start again," instead of being grateful He gave you the tools [TO] start again! Some will complain saying,

"I have to start all over again."

Nevertheless you can say,

"I get to start all over again!"

It Truly Isn't Over Until YOU Win!

"And David said, What have I now done? Is there not a cause? And he turned from him toward another, and spake after the same manner: and the people answered him again after the former manner." (I Samuel 17:29)

"But thanks be to God, which giveth us the victory through our Lord Jesus Christ." (1 Corinthians 15:57)

COPIOUS COURAGE

Trust in the Lord with all thine heart; and lean not unto thine own understanding. (Proverbs 3:5)

YOU CAN GET THERE FROM HERE

Notes and Reflections

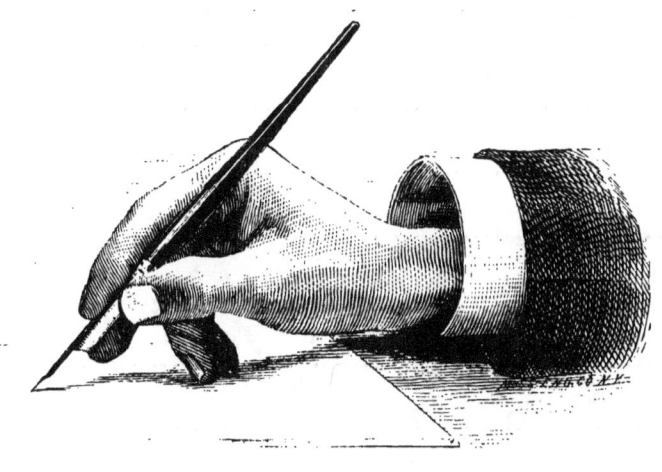

COPIOUS COURAGE

YOU CAN GET THERE FROM HERE

COPIOUS COURAGE

CHAPTER 11
OVERCOMING FEAR & ANXIETY

There are various types of fears. One fear is a reverent fear as in "the fear of the Lord." (Hebrew, *yir'ah*)

"The fear of the LORD is clean, enduring for ever: the judgments of the LORD are true and righteous altogether." (Psalms 19:9)

Fear (Hebrew, *yare'*) to reverence and be in "awe" of. "Thou shalt rise up before the hoary head, and honor the *face of the old man, and fear thy God: I am the LORD."* (Leviticus 19:32)

Generally when we think about a terrifying or dreadful fear, we usually quote 2 Timothy 1:7 "For God hath not given us the spirit of fear; but of power, and of love, and of a sound mind." Nevertheless, the word fear there has nothing to do with being terrified or afraid. The word fear (Greek, *delia*) in this verse means timidity. God does not want us to be cowards or shy, but rather bold. The other fear (Greek, *phobos*) however, is an evil plague that destroys lives. Every minute, every second, someone has been victimized by this terror, this fear.

"When the disciples saw him walking on the lake, they were terrified. "It's a ghost," they said, and cried out in fear." (Matthew 14:26 NIV)

Fear is an enemy of strength because it is the direct opposite of faith.

"And he that doubteth is damned if he eat, because he eateth not of faith: for whatsoever is not of faith is sin." (Romans 14:23)

Where there is fear, there is little faith. Where there is little faith, there is little strength.

It is concerning how fear affects so many lives. How many of us have experienced these popular fears? Tropophobia, Atychiphobia, Thanatophobia, Panthophobia, Algiophobia, Eremiphobia, Socialphobia, Doxophobia, Philophobia, Alophobia, Enissophobia, Decidoophobia, Peniaphobia, Gamophobia. You may say, "I don't have any of these fears in my life." Think again. I have experienced each one personally.

Tropophobia is the fear of moving or fear of change. Metathesiophobia is when this fear becomes extreme to the point of shortness of breath, panic attacks and possible fainting.

We can be creatures of habit who get comfortable in a particular way of existing. This fear had been with me at various times in the past. However, when my wife and I were talking about moving to Florida, I was excited, but then got very ill when I allowed my mind to consider the "what if" in various situations. As I began to rejoice in the Lord, the fear left.

"Now the LORD had said unto Abram, Get thee out of thy country, and from thy kindred, and from thy father's house, unto a land that I will show thee:" (Genesis 12:1)

"Behold, I will do a new thing; now it shall spring forth; shall ye not know it? I will even make a way in the wilderness, and rivers in the desert." (Isaiah 43:19)

Atychiphobia is the fear of failure. Many times with this fear, is also a fear of success. When plagued by the two, you always feel at a standstill or holding pattern in your life.

"Then you will have success if you are careful to observe the decrees and laws that the LORD gave Moses for Israel. Be strong and courageous. Do not be afraid or discouraged." (1 Chronicles 22:13 NIV)

Thanatophobia is the fear of death. I used to hear when I was younger that people who fear death really fear living. As we focus on the life God has made available, we can overcome a fear of death.

"Jesus said unto her, I am the resurrection, and the life: he that believeth in me, though he were dead, yet shall

he live: And whosoever liveth and believeth in me shall never die. Believest thou this?" (John 11:25-26)

"O death, where is thy sting? O grave, where is thy victory?" (1 Corinthians 15:55)

Panthophobia is the fear of sickness and disease.

"Bless the LORD, O my soul, and forget not all his benefits: Who forgiveth all thine iniquities; who healeth all thy diseases;" (Psalms 103:2)

Algiophobia is the fear of pain. Some fear sickness because they fear pain.

"For we have not an high priest which cannot be touched with the feeling of our infirmities; but was in all points tempted like as we are, yet without sin." (Hebrews 4:15)

Eremiphobia is the fear of being alone. When people feel alone, most Christians quote Hebrews 14:5. "…He will never leave you nor forsake you." Yet, they themselves are surrounded by family, friends, and support. I think we agree and understand the precious covenant of the Lord. However, we were made into flesh. I heard Pastor Linda Rowan once say, "Sometimes you need encouragement by someone with flesh on." God has called us also to be there for one another.

"Not forsaking the assembling of ourselves together, as the manner of some is; but exhorting one another: and so much the more, as ye see the day approaching." (Hebrews 10:25)

Socialphobia is the fear of people, their rejection, opinions, and views.

"Have not I commanded thee? Be strong and of a good courage; be not afraid, neither be thou dismayed: for the LORD thy God is with thee whithersoever thou goest." (Joshua 1:9)

"In God have I put my trust: I will not be afraid what man can do unto me." (Psalms 56:11)

Doxophobia is the fear of expressing yourself or opinions.

*"I am the LORD thy God, which brought thee out of the

land of Egypt: open thy mouth wide, and I will fill it."* (Psalms 81:10)

Philophobia is the fear of love or being in love. I used to fear love for I did not know what love was. It may sound elementary, but it is true. God is love. Our fear for Him is reverence, not terror.

"There is no fear in love; but perfect love casteth out fear: because fear hath torment. He that feareth is not made perfect in love." (1 John 4:18)

Altophobia is the fear of heights. Acrophobia is when the fear becomes extreme.

Wherever we are, we are not out of the care, reach, or love of Almighty God.

"For I am persuaded, that neither death, nor life, nor angels, nor principalities, nor powers, nor things present, nor things to come, Nor height, nor depth, nor any other creature, shall be able to separate us from the love of God, which is in Christ Jesus our Lord." (Romans 8:38-39)

"...when men are afraid of heights and of dangers in the streets; when the almond tree blossoms and the grasshopper drags himself along and desire no longer is stirred." (Ecclesiastes 12:5)

Enissophobia is the fear of criticism. Constructive criticism is necessary for healthy living. I used to hate being challenged as if everything I said or did was right in my own eyes. I am no longer an insecure kid, defending my erroneous ways at all cost. Don't fear man's opinions, but consider truth when presented with it.

"To one who listens, valid criticism is like a gold earring or other gold jewelry."
(Proverbs 25:12 New Living Translation)

"If you ignore criticism, you will end in poverty and disgrace; if you accept correction, you will be honored."
(Proverbs 13:18 New Living Translation)

Decidophobia is the fear of making decisions. If we consult God in every decision, we no longer have to fear making wrong choices. Wrong choices are usually made when we do not seek wise counsel.

With proper accountability, fear will go.

"Where no counsel is, the people fall: but in the multitude of counsellors there is safety." (Proverbs 11:14)

"My son, do not forget my teaching, but keep my commands in your heart, for they will prolong your life many years and bring you prosperity. Let love and faithfulness never leave you; bind them around your neck, write them on the tablet of your heart. Then you will win favor and a good name in the sight of God and man. Trust in the LORD with all your heart and lean not on your own understanding; in all your ways acknowledge him, and he will make your paths straight. Do not be wise in your own eyes; fear the LORD and shun evil." (Proverbs 3:1-7)

Peniaphobia is the fear of poverty. Many people don't support the work of Christ on a level they are able, out of a fear of being broke.

Gamophobia is the fear of marriage. Marriage is an honorable thing, and God wants to bless you with a spouse you can love. Wait and seek out God's best for you.

These fears, although common, can be overcome with proper instruction and care. There is strength available for each fear we face.

"And God shall wipe away all tears from their eyes; and there shall be no more death, neither sorrow, nor crying, neither shall there be any more pain: for the former things are passed away." (Revelation 21:4)

"Fear thou not; for I am with thee: be not dismayed; for I am thy God: I will strengthen thee; yea, I will help thee; yea, I will uphold thee with the right hand of my righteousness." (Isaiah 41:10)

With each fear we overcome, new strength is revealed through us. I am a living witness, I am an overcomer. We have a bible full of those who rose above these challenges and walked in greatness before their God.

OVERCOMING FEAR AND ANXIETY

Notes and Reflections

OVERCOMING FEAR AND ANXIETY

COPIOUS COURAGE

CHAPTER 12
COURAGE TO LIVE, COURAGE TO DIE, COURAGE TO CHANGE

Many reading this book will take away keys to living a courageous life. Indeed, life takes courage. It takes courage to live the life God intended for us from the beginning.

"The thief does not come except to steal, and to kill, and to destroy. I have come that they may have life, and that

they may have it more abundantly." (John 10:10)

Abundant living is not some life of fame or fortune. It is a life of complete satisfaction knowing the love and grace of God in everyday life. Prosperity is more than money. Prosperity involves wealth of resources, mental and physical wellness, and healthy relationships with others. It takes courage to live when odds are stacked up against you.

About 1 in 8 U.S. women (about 12%) will develop invasive breast cancer over the course of her lifetime. In 2020, an estimated 276,480 new cases of invasive breast cancer are expected to be diagnosed in women in the U.S., along with 48,530 new cases of non-invasive (in situ) breast cancer. About 2,620 new cases of invasive breast cancer are expected to be diagnosed in men in 2020. About 42,170 women in the U.S. are expected to die in 2020 from breast cancer.

Regardless of these numbers, thousands of women who have been diagnosed with cancer yet attend college. Many continue to work jobs, raise families, and serve God and their communities. They confront the odds. They have hope for a tomorrow; they all have courage to live.

Currently, there are almost 2,500 inmates on death row. Some have decided to utilize their time being angry, tearing up letters and refusing any visitors. Yet, hundreds read and write books. Many learn new trades and obtain degrees. Some entertain each other as well as the guards. There were a handful that did television interviews with smiles on their faces and profound wisdom coming out of their mouths.

These individuals, regardless of their sad reality, have decided to live. What is our excuse?
If we can move our justifications and excuses to the side, and humbly see the world around us, we can experience LIFE.

Just Die Already

The born again experience teaches us the concept of rebirth. It is in rebirth that we welcome death knowing a resurrection and newness is made available to us. In relationship to this, some can't live because they simply refuse to die. If we can just die already, we can live. I pray we die to our stupid thinking and immature ways. We don't have to mess up and always learn from our own mistakes. We do much better learning from the mistakes of others. It takes courage to die and to experience the new birth once and for all.

Therefore if any man be in Christ, he is a new creature: old things are passed away; behold, all things are become new. (2 Corinthians 5:17)

(The Prayer of Francis of Assisi)

"Lord, make me an instrument of your peace,
Where there is hatred, let me sow love;
Where there is injury, pardon;
Where there is doubt, faith;
Where there is despair, hope;
Where there is darkness, light;
Where there is sadness, joy;
 O Divine Master,
Grant that I may not so much seek
To be consoled as to console;
To be understood as to understand;
To be loved as to love.
For it is in giving that we receive;
It is in pardoning that we are pardoned;
And it is in dying that we are born to eternal life."

A Change Is A Change

To be honest, I'm no longer looking for "a wonderful change." I will take any change at this point. I come to realize that every change doesn't have to be wonderful, just necessary. If every change was so wonderful more people would buy into it. Don't get me wrong. There are those who have experienced amazing change and it was sure enough wonderful.

I too, can testify to the awesomeness of Almighty God and how He comes in and changes us. Everything He does is marvelous, amazing, and wonderful. However, your next change may come out of desperation. You may have to cry one in, and cry one out. No worries, He'll make it wonderful soon enough—but for now, just be grateful for the change.

"Don't wait until everything is just right. It will never be perfect. There will always be challenges, obstacles and less than perfect conditions. So what. Get started now. With each step you take, you will grow stronger and stronger, more and more skilled, more and more self-confident and more and more successful."
—Mark Victor Hansen

Say out loud, "Lord, I want to live, I want to die, I want to change!"

COURAGE TO LIVE, COURAGE TO DIE, COURAGE TO CHANGE

Notes and Reflections

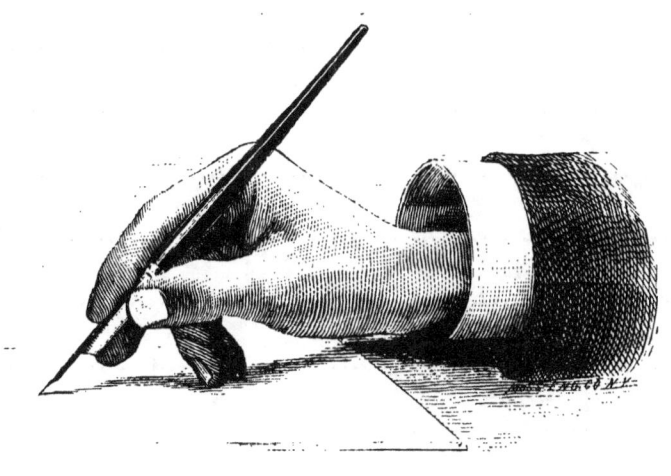

COURAGE TO LIVE, COURAGE TO DIE, COURAGE TO CHANGE

....
....
....
....
....
....
....
....
....
....
....
....
....
....
....
....
....
....
....
....
....
....
....
....
....

COPIOUS COURAGE

Verses To Help You Every Day!

Strength

"I can do all things through him who strengthens me." (Philippians 4:13)

"Fear not, for I am with you; be not dismayed, for I am your God; I will strengthen you, I will help you, I will uphold you with my righteous right hand." (Isaiah 41:10)

"Be strong and courageous. Do not fear or be in dread of them, for it is the Lord your God who goes with you. He will not leave you or forsake you." (Deuteronomy 31:6)

"But they who wait for the Lord shall renew their strength; they shall mount up with wings like eagles; they shall run and not be weary; they shall walk and not faint." (Isaiah 40:31)

"No temptation has overtaken you that is not common to man. God is faithful, and he will not let you be tempted beyond your ability, but with the temptation he will also provide the way of escape, that you may be able to endure it."
(1 Corinthians 10:13)

"The Lord is my strength and my song, and he has become my salvation; this is my God, and I will praise him, my father's God, and I will exalt him." (Exodus 15:2)

"Finally, be strong in the Lord and in the strength of his might." (Ephesians 6:10)

"For the Lord your God is he who goes with you to fight for you against your enemies, to give you the victory." (Deuteronomy 20:4)

"But he said to me, "My grace is sufficient for you, for my power is made perfect in weakness."

Therefore I will boast all the more gladly of my weaknesses, so that the power of Christ may rest upon me. For the sake of Christ, then, I am content with weaknesses, insults, hardships, persecutions, and calamities.

For when I am weak, then I am strong." (2 Corinthians 12:9-10)

"Have I not commanded you? Be strong and

courageous. Do not be frightened, and do not be dismayed, for the Lord your God is with you wherever you go." (Joshua 1:9)

"For God gave us a spirit not of fear but of power and love and self-control." (2 Timothy 1:7)

"Behold, God is my salvation; I will trust, and will not be afraid; for the Lord God is my strength and my song, and he has become my salvation." (Isaiah 12:2)

"He gives power to the faint, and to him who has no might he increases strength." (Isaiah 40:29)

"The Lord is my light and my salvation; whom shall I fear? The Lord is the stronghold of my life; of whom shall I be afraid?" (Psalm 27:1)

"Be strong, and let your heart take courage, all you who wait for the Lord!" (Psalm 31:24)

"My flesh and my heart may fail, but God is the strength of my heart and my portion forever." (Psalm 73:26)

"But he said to me, "My grace is sufficient for you, for my power is made perfect in weakness." Therefore I will boast all the more gladly of my weaknesses, so that the power of Christ may rest upon me."
(2 Corinthians 12:9)

"And you shall love the Lord your God with all your heart and with all your soul and with all your mind and with all your strength." (Mark 12:30)

"God is our refuge and strength, a very present help in trouble." (Psalm 46:1)

"May the Lord give strength to his people! May the Lord bless his people with peace." (Psalm 29:11)

"I have said these things to you, that in me you may have peace. In the world you will have tribulation. But take heart; I have overcome the world."
(John 16:33)

"But seek first the kingdom of God and his righteousness, and all these things will be added to you." (Matthew 6:33)

"Even though I walk through the valley of the shadow of death, I will fear no evil, for you are with me; your rod and your staff, they comfort me." (Psalm 23:4)

"The Lord is my strength and my song; he has become my salvation." (Psalm 118:14)

Verses To Help You Every Day!

Faith

Faith is what gives us the courage to keep going when we feel overwhelmed. It is through faith in God that we can trust in His goodness. These Scripture quotes teach us the power of God that is available to us when we have faith!

"For nothing will be impossible with God."
(Luke 1:37)

"For by grace you have been saved through faith. And this is not your own doing; it is the gift of God, not a result of works, so that no one may boast."
(Ephesians 2:8-9)

"Trust in the Lord with all your heart, and do not lean on your own understanding. In all your ways acknowledge him, and he will make straight your paths." (Proverbs 3:5-6)

"For we walk by faith, not by sight."
(2 Corinthians 5:7)

"And Jesus answered them, 'Truly, I say to you, if you have faith and do not doubt, you will not only do what has been done to the fig tree, but even if you say

to this mountain, 'Be taken up and thrown into the sea,' it will happen. And whatever you ask in prayer, you will receive, if you have faith."
(Matthew 21:21-22)

"And without faith it is impossible to please him, for whoever would draw near to God must believe that he exists and that he rewards those who seek him." (Hebrews 11:6)

"Now faith is the assurance of things hoped for, the conviction of things not seen." (Hebrews 11:1)

"And Jesus answered them, "Have faith in God. Truly, I say to you, whoever says to this mountain, 'Be taken up and thrown into the sea,' and does not doubt in his heart, but believes that what he says will come to pass, it will be done for him. Therefore I tell you, whatever you ask in prayer, believe that you have received it, and it will be yours." (Mark 11:22-24)

"Though you have not seen him, you love him. Though you do not now see him, you believe in him and rejoice with joy that is inexpressible and filled with glory, obtaining the outcome of your faith, the salvation of your souls." (1 Peter 1:8-9)

"May you be strengthened with all power, according to his glorious might, for all endurance and patience with joy," (Colossians 1:11)

"But let all who take refuge in you rejoice; let them ever sing for joy, and spread your protection over them, that those who love your name may exult in you." (Psalm 5:11)

"You have turned for me my mourning into dancing; you have loosed my sackcloth and clothed me with gladness," (Psalm 30:11)

"Splendor and majesty are before him; strength and joy are in his place." (1 Chronicles 16:27)

Verses To Help You Every Day!

Dealing with Fear

God does not want us to fear anything in life because He already won the victory over evil and death. While we may momentarily feel anxieties rise, we can be reminded by these Bible verses that we can trade our worries for joy.

"Peace I leave with you; my peace I give to you. Not as the world gives do I give to you. Let not your hearts be troubled, neither let them be afraid." (John 14:27)

"The LORD is my light and my salvation—whom shall I fear? The LORD is the stronghold of my life—of whom shall I be afraid?" (Psalm 27:1)

"Therefore do not worry about tomorrow, for tomorrow will worry about itself. Each day has enough trouble of its own." (Matthew 6:34)

"Rejoice in hope, be patient in tribulation, be constant in prayer." (Romans 12:12)

"But now, this is what the LORD says—he who created you, Jacob, he who formed you, Israel: "Do not fear, for I have redeemed you; I have summoned you by name; you are mine." (Isaiah 43:1)

"I sought the LORD, and he answered me; he delivered me from all my fears." (Psalm 34:4)

"When anxiety was great within me, your consolation brought me joy." (Psalm 94:19)

"Rejoice in the Lord always; again I will say, Rejoice." (Philippians 4:4)

"But the fruit of the Spirit is love, joy, peace, patience, kindness, goodness, faithfulness," (Galatians 5:22)

"Until now you have asked nothing in my name. Ask, and you will receive, that your joy may be full." (John 16:24)

"A joyful heart is good medicine, but a crushed spirit dries up the bones." (Proverbs 17:22)

"Though you have not seen him, you love him. Though you do not now see him, you believe in him and rejoice with joy that is inexpressible and filled with glory," (1 Peter 1:8)

"So also you have sorrow now, but I will see you again, and your hearts will rejoice, and no one will take your joy from you." (John 16:22)

"This is the day that the Lord has made; let us rejoice and be glad in it." (Psalm 118:24)

"You make known to me the path of life; in your presence there is fullness of joy; at your right hand are pleasures forevermore." (Psalm 16:11)

"These things I have spoken to you, that my joy may be in you, and that your joy may be full." (John 15:11)

"For his anger is but for a moment, and his favor is for a lifetime. Weeping may tarry for the night, but joy comes with the morning." (Psalm 30:5)

"Therefore my heart is glad, and my whole being rejoices; my flesh also dwells secure." (Psalm 16:9)

"Rejoice always, pray without ceasing, give thanks in all circumstances; for this is the will of God in Christ Jesus for you." (1 Thessalonians 5:16-18)

"For you shall go out in joy and be led forth in peace; the mountains and the hills before you shall break forth into singing, and all the trees of the field shall clap their hands." (Isaiah 55:12)

Verses To Help You Every Day!
Healing

"Heal me, O Lord, and I will be healed; save me and I will be saved, for you are the one I praise." (Jeremiah 17:14)

"Is anyone among you sick? Let them call the elders of the church to pray over them and anoint them with oil in the name of the Lord. And the prayer offered in faith will make the sick person well; the Lord will raise them up." (James 5:14-15)

He said, "If you listen carefully to the LORD your God and do what is right in his eyes, if you pay attention to his commands and keep all his decrees, I will not bring on you any of the diseases I brought on the Egyptians, for I am the LORD, who heals you." (Exodus 15:26)

"Worship the LORD your God, and his blessing will be on your food and water. I will take away sickness from among you…" (Exodus 23:25)

"…I am with you; do not be dismayed, for I am your God. I will strengthen you and help you; I will uphold you with my righteous right hand." (Isaiah 41:10)

"Surely he took up our pain and bore our suffering, yet we considered him punished by God, stricken by him, and afflicted. But he was pierced for our transgressions, he was crushed for our iniquities; the punishment that brought us peace was on him, and by his wounds we are healed." (Isaiah 53:4-5)

"But I will restore you to health and heal your wounds,' declares the LORD" (Jeremiah 30:17)

"See now that I myself am he! There is no god besides me. I put to death and I bring to life, I have wounded and I will heal, and no one can deliver out of my hand." (Deuteronomy 32:39)

"If my people, who are called by my name, will humble themselves and pray and seek my face and turn from their wicked ways, then I will hear from heaven, and I will forgive their sin and will heal their land. Now my eyes will be open and my ears attentive to the prayers offered in this place." (2 Chronicles 7:14-15)

"You restored me to health and let me live. Surely it was for my benefit that I suffered such anguish. In your love you kept me from the pit of destruction; you have put all my sins behind your back." (Isaiah 38:16-17)

"I have seen their ways, but I will heal them; I will guide them and restore comfort to Israel's mourners, creating praise on their lips. Peace, peace, to those far and near," says the LORD. "And I will heal them." (Isaiah 57:18-19)

"Nevertheless, I will bring health and healing to it; I will heal my people and will let them enjoy abundant peace and security." (Jeremiah 33:6)

"Dear friend, I pray that you may enjoy good health and that all may go well with you, even as your soul is getting along well." (3 John 1:2)

"He will wipe every tear from their eyes. There will be no more death or mourning or crying or pain, for the old order of things has passed away." (Revelations 21:4)

Final Notes and Reflections

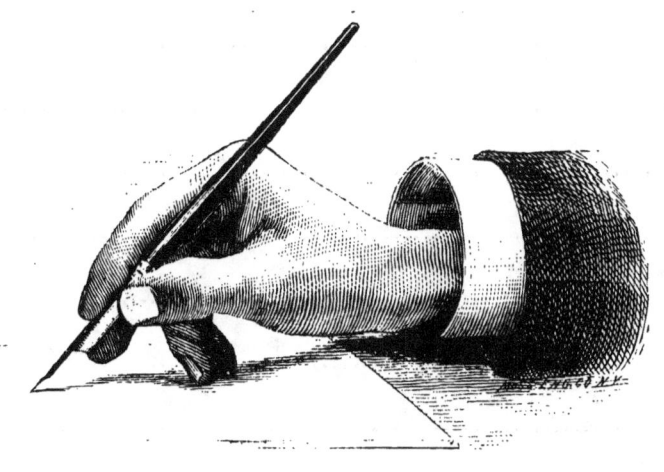

For I know the thoughts that I think toward you, saith the Lord, thoughts of peace, and not of evil, to give you an expected end. (Jeremiah 29:11)

www.ingramcontent.com/pod-product-compliance
Lightning Source LLC
Chambersburg PA
CBHW070601010526
44118CB00012B/1407